Uncertain Saints

Uncertain Saints

Poems and Prayers for Wrestling with God

CARSON CAWTHON MATTHEWS

RESOURCE *Publications* • Eugene, Oregon

UNCERTAIN SAINTS
Poems and Prayers for Wrestling with God

Copyright © 2025 Carson Cawthon Matthews. All rights reserved. Except for brief quotations in critical publications or reviews, no part of this book may be reproduced in any manner without prior written permission from the publisher. Write: Permissions, Wipf and Stock Publishers, 199 W. 8th Ave., Suite 3, Eugene, OR 97401.

Resource Publications
An Imprint of Wipf and Stock Publishers
199 W. 8th Ave., Suite 3
Eugene, OR 97401

www.wipfandstock.com

PAPERBACK ISBN: 979-8-3852-4024-1
HARDCOVER ISBN: 979-8-3852-4025-8
EBOOK ISBN: 979-8-3852-4026-5

VERSION NUMBER 051925

For my nine-year-old self.
Light is returning everything the darkness stole.

The opposite of faith is not doubt, but certainty. Certainty is missing the point entirely. Faith includes noticing the mess, the emptiness and discomfort, and letting it be there until some light returns.
— Anne Lamott, *Plan B: Further Thoughts on Faith*

Contents

Acknowledgments | ix
Introduction | xi

The Great Litany (For Uncertain Saints) | 1

Eat My Flesh | 5

Old Dreams | 6

Santorini Cathedral, Monday Afternoon | 7

Holy Saturday | 8

Mother Tongue | 9

Women's History | 10

Body Economy | 11

Performative Girlhood | 12

How To Stay Home | 13

Burning Witches | 14

Feminist | 15

Annunciation | 16

Rainstick | 17

Jesus wept. | 18

Nourishment | 19

Starve the Flesh | 20

Well Rounded | 21

Creed for My Body | 22

Confession of My Prior Certainty | 23

Genesis | 24

False Gods | 25

Tough Love | 26

Gloria in Excelsis | 27

Church of the Water Falling | 28

Sanctus | 29

Women's Work | 30

No Christ But In Things | 31

Love, Again | 32

Be Fruitful and Multiply | 33

Sabbath | 34

Acknowledgments

IN THE WORDS OF Mr. Fred Rogers, "All of us have special ones who have loved us into being." There are so many people in my life who have made me who I am today, and I am forever grateful.

To begin, thank you to Wipf and Stock and my editor Matthew Wimer for bringing this book to life. It is my wildest dream come true. Thanks also to Hannah Gaskamp for designing this stunning cover.

Thank you to all of the journals that originally published these poems, including *The Ivy Leaves Journal of Literature and Art*, *Calf Magazine*, *Glass Mountain Magazine*, *The Penwood Review*, *The Opal*, *Calla Press*, *Pensive Journal*, *The Unmooring*, *Fallow House*, *The Clayjar Review*, and *The Way Back to Ourselves*.

Thank you to Lily McNamara, who workshopped this book with me. I think you're a genius. Thank you also to my dear friends who read countless versions of this book and offered invaluable feedback: Emma Miller, Maggie Wilson, Ryleigh Wallace, Chloe Wallace, Sydney Himpel, and Alexandra Oliver.

I am forever grateful to every teacher who has taught me to love writing; this book doesn't exist without you. Special thanks to Mrs. Dubose, Mrs. Goldstein (Mayer), Mrs. Hofler, and Dr. Wyma.

Thank you to the saints at Newspring Florence, Christ Reformed, and the Church of the Ascension who allowed me to borrow faith when I had none. You couldn't be more different from one another, but you've each taught me to see goodness, truth, and beauty more clearly.

Acknowledgments

To my friends from the Rocky's Hot Chicken group chat: Thank you for filling the last five years with so much laughter. Does anyone want to come over and play Quiplash?

To Jordan Danford Melgar, my oldest friend. I'm so grateful to grow up beside you.

To Anna Reese, my second sister. On one of the worst days of my life, you took care of me, no questions asked. You were a safe place for me, and you still are. "Rainstick" is for you.

Thank you to the Matthews family, for welcoming me into your lives so wholeheartedly.

Thank you to all four of my grandparents. Your faithfulness and legacy inspire me every day.

Dad, thank you for teaching me that I can do anything I set my mind to. I've never had to wonder if you're proud of me.

Mom, thank you for teaching me how to be a woman and a writer. You are a badass.

Campbell, you're the only one who's been beside me for the whole story. I want to be more like you when I grow up.

Jared, my favorite adventure began the day I met you. Loving you and being loved by you is my greatest accomplishment. You are kinder, gentler, and more patient than I dared to dream a husband could be. I love you.

And, finally, to the King of Kings, Love Incarnate: You're better than I ever imagined. All of this is for You. Amen.

Introduction

IN FOURTH GRADE, I stopped sleeping. I was an otherwise healthy nine-year-old little girl, with loving parents and a safe home environment. But, every night as I laid my head on the pillow, I was plagued with violent, scary, and repulsive intrusive thoughts. The more I struggled against them, the stronger they became. My parents didn't know how to help me, and doctors didn't have a diagnosis. We tried everything. I ran miles a day, hoping the physical exertion would be enough to help me fall into bed at night. I took sleep supplements religiously, far more than any child should. I posted Scripture above my pillow, recited dozens of verses before bed, and my parents prayed over me faithfully. Still, come 3 am, I would remain wide awake weeping into my pillow, haunted by the images on a loop in my brain. I was scared of myself, convinced the thoughts and images were reflective of my true character, that I was a deeply depraved person and a danger to society. Relief did not come for many more years. But there was one trick, one treatment we tried, that would temporarily alleviate my suffering: reading.

Each evening, as the dread of another sleepless night settled into my gut, I picked up a book and began to read. I imagined that, by reading, I was borrowing someone else's thoughts for a while, when I desperately needed a break from my own. I read anything I could get my hands on: children's books from school, my dad's books on business, my mom's Christian nonfiction, and trivia books meant to be read on the toilet. Aside from whatever

INTRODUCTION

paperbacks I found lying around, I also read large chunks of the Bible at a time. I had a pension for the Psalms, because David wrote of so many sleepless nights, and the Levitical law because I loved the embodied aspects of faith. Beth Moore, John Grisham, and Moses served as my companions for many long nights. I came to treasure these books so much that I took to sleeping with them tucked under my pillow. I hoped that the author's thoughts would overpower my own by some strange osmosis, and, sometimes, it worked. If ever I was able to drift to sleep peacefully during those years, it was because I was imagining words from the page played out behind my eyelids.

After seven years of this routine, I was diagnosed with severe Obsessive Compulsive Disorder as a sophomore in high school. I started taking medication, found a psychiatrist, and cycled through a whole host of therapists. At last, the fog began to clear a bit. I had a name for what I was experiencing and a community of professionals who assured me I wasn't crazy. Best of all, I started sleeping again.

I still experience intrusive thoughts every single day, and Obsessive Compulsive Disorder is still very much a part of my life. I still take medication, see a psychiatrist, and engage in Exposure Response Prevention (ERP) therapy, which is the gold standard for OCD treatment. I probably will continue doing all three of those things until I die, and I'm ok with that. This is part of my story now.

It has been fourteen years since I first experienced symptoms of OCD as a nine-year-old girl, but, through all fourteen years, one habit has stuck around: I'm still an avid reader. Reading is an integral part of my way of life, and I have even come to view it as a spiritual practice.

During those long, anxious nights as a child, I prayed often. I begged God to remove the thoughts from my mind, to heal me, to give me an answer. For those seven years, it seemed like God was silent on the issue. What kind of God would abandon His child to this kind of distress? It seemed cruel.

Introduction

As I have reflected on those years of untreated OCD, I have come to understand that those books I read late into the night were a tangible form of God's presence with me. The Bible, Christian nonfiction, and even fairy tales or joke books became a physical manifestation of God's grace for me, providing comfort and allowing me to borrow a story other than my own for a while. Those authors were doing God's work, whether they meant to or not. And even on the darkest nights, God was there with me. God was present in those pages, and God was answering my prayers.

I wrestled with God because of my mental illness, but there are countless other reasons why you may enter your own season of doubt. This book is for anyone who has ever felt relegated to the margins of their spiritual community because of their suffering, anyone who has ever felt like there is no one to hold space for their story. These poems and prayers are yours to borrow until you find your voice again.

Books are an integral part of my spiritual practice now. I encounter God every day through reading the Bible, praying the Psalms, and reflecting on the Book of Common Prayer, and you will find all three reflected in this book's poems and prayers.

I believe that honest, raw portrayals of the human experience can heal us and remind us that we are not alone. Therefore, this book contains some profanity and references to mature topics, including sexual assault, mental illness, and eating disorders. If reading about these topics would be more harmful than healing for you, I encourage you to skip ahead whenever necessary.

I hope these words meet you in the middle of your story, while you continue to wrestle with God. If this book keeps you company in your own uncertainty, then I'll have done all I set out to do.

Under the mercy,
Carson Cawthon Matthews

The Great Litany (For Uncertain Saints)

O God the Father, kind and gracious Creator,
Have mercy on us.

O God the Son, carpenter and King,
Have mercy on us.

O God the Holy Spirit, Gardener of our hearts,
Have mercy on us.

O holy, blessed, and glorious Trinity, one God,
Have mercy on us.

Forgive us, Lord Jesus, for when we have sought to impede Your image in ourselves, each other, and your world. Spare us, good Lord, from knowing days outside of your love's light.
Spare us, good Lord.

From losing the thread of our own stories, and from forgetting your kindnesses to us in days past,
Good Lord, deliver us.

From absurd promises of certainty and a lack of curiosity,
Good Lord, deliver us.

From a version of Your Gospel contaminated with a love for power,
Good Lord, deliver us.

From hatred of our neighbors, and the hypocrisy that so easily entangles,
Good Lord, deliver us.

From a faith so rigid it leaves no room for You,
Good Lord, deliver us.

From believing we are the heroes of our own stories,
Good Lord, deliver us.

From a salvation that is only for the Westerners, the rich, or the white,
Good Lord, deliver us.

From the idolization of autonomy,
Good Lord, deliver us.

From heresies which minimize the power of Your Word,
Good Lord, deliver us.

From the love of knowledge paired with a lack of action,
Good Lord, deliver us.

From an understanding of Scripture devoid of context,
Good Lord, deliver us.

From a Christian narrative which minimizes Christ's suffering,
Good Lord, deliver us.

By the miracle of Your Incarnation, Your human life, Your feasting, and your fasting,
Good Lord, deliver us.

By the mercy of Your death, Your public execution for our sake,
Good Lord, deliver us.

By Your resurrection on the third day, and the promise that darkness will not reign forever,
Good Lord, deliver us.

In all times and all places, for all of Your people and Your creation, in birth and in death, in weeping and in laughter, in mourning and in dancing, in seeking and in losing, in love and in hate, in war and in peace,
Good Lord, deliver us.

We, saints through the death, resurrection, and ascension of our Lord Jesus Christ, beseech you to hear us, O God, that it might please you to work Your mission through us.
We beseech you to hear us, Good Lord.

That it may please thee to grant us a good and beautiful language around our faith, so we may praise You with Your own words.
We beseech you to hear us, Good Lord.

That it may please thee to tend gently to those arrested by a dizzying uncertainty, that they may find themselves held by Your faithful love.
We beseech you to hear us, Good Lord.

That it may please thee to teach us to live the culturally upside-down narrative of the Bible in our own contexts.
We beseech you to hear us, Good Lord.

That it may please thee to allow us the space and time to make mistakes, knowing that You will catch us when we fall.
We beseech you to hear us, Good Lord.

That it may please thee to cause us to remember our own humanity, that we would become ever more aware of your gentleness towards us.
We beseech you to hear us, Good Lord.

That it may please thee to place us in communities that help us interpret your Word, and that we may become better neighbors in the process.
We beseech you to hear us, Good Lord.

That it may please thee to place people in our lives who can faithfully imagine a better future for us, even before we can imagine it for ourselves.
We beseech you to hear us, Good Lord.

That it may please thee to establish patterns of Christian practice in our lives, so we may practice our way into a more wholehearted knowledge of You.
We beseech you to hear us, Good Lord.

That it may please thee to give us eyes to see You in all the beauty of the Earth.
We beseech you to hear us, Good Lord.

That it may please thee to uphold Your Church and all her members.
We beseech you to hear us, Good Lord.

That it may please thee to return everything the darkness stole from us by the power of Your Light.
We beseech you to hear us, Good Lord.

Son of God, we beseech you to hear us.
Son of God, we beseech you to hear us.

O suffering servant, you take away the sin of the world.
Have mercy on us.

O suffering servant, you take away the sin of the world.
Have mercy on us.

O suffering servant, you take away the sin of the world.
Grant us your peace.

O Christ, hear us.
O Christ, hear us.

Lord, have mercy upon us.
Christ, have mercy upon us.
Lord, have mercy upon us.

Eat My Flesh

When I was baptized at age ten
I dwelled not on any blessed salvation,

my thoughts were consumed by countless skin cells
adrift in that holy water,
above me and all around me.

Pieces of the people gone before me
into this sacred pool
in which I live and move and have my being.

Still,
I squeezed my eyes shut, held my breath.
Praying I'd be counted with
The Righteous.

As an adult, I call it OCD.

As a child, I called it Faith.

Old Dreams

Thrift stores always manage to have
that particular Thrift Store Smell:

Eau de deflated soccer ball,
musk of ex-boyfriend's jacket,
and chipped mug tinted slightly brown,
smelling of grubby coins.

A used gumball machine beside
a painting of Jesus, pale face pulled taut in a grimace,
haunted by memories of his Father's house.

and just a whiff of seance
with oddly quiet ghosts.

Santorini Cathedral, Monday Afternoon

The heat is angry, gritty.
We tuck into a church,
hungrily, light a candle like
a prayer, give thanks for the shade the saints provide,
smelling sweat and melted wax.
The man over my left
shoulder wears a Miller Lite
T-shirt. He wipes his dripping forehead
with the hem, his hands sticky with
melted gelato. Behind him, Mary Magdalene's
left incisor, gilded. The ceiling like a prayer shawl,
protecting wrinkled skin from Grecian sun.

The man looks up, whispers, *"damn."*

Holy Saturday

O God of Gethsemane,
Teach us to wait for you.

We approach you, half-dust and half-spirit,
knowing we dwell in the already and the not-yet.
Help us to wait well.

We know it is not a sin to want,
because of your son
who prayed: *Let this cup pass from me.*
Let us follow his example.

Grant us the perseverance to continue in prayer,
that on the day when heaven meets Earth,
we may not be found sleeping.

Teach us to grieve what is broken in this world,
and assure us that our grief may never separate us from you.

In the name of God the Crucified, Jesus Christ, we pray.

Amen.

Mother Tongue

My mother taught me to
raise the dead regularly,
gave me a gospel of salt and
blood, calloused hands and
strange fire.

Her prayers over me smell of tobacco
and spill like commandments:
"Thou shalt not confess to nice boys
with serpent tongues and eager
hands.

Thou shalt not find yourself
on your knees again."

Women's History

Our mothers and their mothers spoke
through quilt stitches,
covering my bare shoulders still.

They served stories steeped and sweetened
after lining their puckered lips in
blood red.

Their history lies sleeping still
in family Bibles
and the slurred diatribes
stumbling from the lips of the men
who used to love them.

Body Economy

An object is worth
whatever someone is
willing to sacrifice
to obtain it.

I wonder how many
women never felt
permission to like their
bodies unless someone
else wanted it
first.

Performative Girlhood

No, *mom*
I can't come down for dinner right now.
It's not my fault that you don't understand.

I'm performing my adolescence
for my loyal audience
of middle-aged men.

How To Stay Home

Bury your feet in soft dirt,
stubborn, until you find your footprints
have become your home's foundation.

Paint the kitchen white
again, again. Bury every lede.

And pray
and pray
and pray
you will not wonder
what could have been.

Burning Witches

When I was a girl someone
told me always yell "fire!"
instead of "rape!"

People are more likely to help,
they said,
if they feel they, too,
are in danger.

This building is on fire.
Our sisters walk its halls.
We turn our heads to the sky
and wonder
why the air smells of smoke.

Feminist

"Who says girls can't do it all?"

"Who says they have to?"

Annunciation

Blessed are those perplexed by the Word of God,
for Christ shall draw near to them.

Blessed are those who are afraid,
for Christ shall be magnified through them.

Blessed are those overshadowed by the Most High,
for they shall be called holy.

Blessed are those who find companionship in suffering,
for they shall leap for joy.

Blessed are those on the fringes of faith,
for Christ shall exalt them.

Blessed are those with souls pierced by swords,
for they shall see resurrection.

And blessed are the God-bearers
who have believed
in a God who bleeds,
for they will inherit the upside-down Kingdom
and worship the unexpected King.

Rainstick

Historically, rain sticks were used to mimic the sound of rain, reminding the gods of human thirst and the peoples' need for supernatural intervention.

We sat on your porch
when you told me all the creative ways
life had found
of breaking your heart.

You didn't even have to say them out loud.
I heard them in the lump in your throat
and the sound of rain on a tin roof.

Jesus wept.

The church doesn't know
how to react
when this too shall last,
doesn't know what to say
when the cup doesn't pass.

We remember Gethsemane.
We know how his eyes welled.

Just because you're hurting
doesn't mean you aren't held.

Nourishment

Starving beast inside a girl
raving, begging for release
I know for sure she'd change the world
if only she would eat

Starve the Flesh

I am twenty years old today
and I want a chocolate cake,

with the boldness to pick a fry off my boyfriend's plate,
and the audacity to tell my hairdresser I hate my haircut
instead of crying in the car.

But more than anything, I want to stop
fearing the depth of my desire.

I'm so tired of believing
it's impolite to be hungry.

I'm no hedonist,
just a girl with an empty stomach
and a mouth choked in prayer,
breathing and pleading,
"I shall not want."

Well Rounded

Thigh-sculpting
Women carved, stuffed, and prepped
to be devoured like Thanksgiving turkeys.

How wild it would be for her
to rejoice in the ways her thighs touch,
tucked close together
like hands clasped
in prayer.

Creed for My Body

I believe in God the Father Almighty,
maker of my body and your body,
and in Jesus Christ
who became the flesh to redeem the flesh.

I have been loved into being,
born into bondage,
freed by the Incarnate,
redeemed,
restored,
and made whole.

The Divine has made His dwelling with me.

Now, I am learning a new way to be human
in my body and in The Body.

I believe in the innate Eros of human nature,
The Logos who writes life,
The Cosmos that heals chaos,
The community of the Trinity,
The commonality of prayer,
and the absolute absurdity of unconditional love.

Amen.

Confession of My Prior Certainty

Almighty God, Great Reconciler, teach us to know you in the tension, those liminal spaces that tempt our human hearts to seek an impossible certainty.

We acknowledge that we are all pilgrims and exiles, and we exist in a state of transience as we await your return.

Grant us the spiritual discipline of curiosity while we wait, and make us wary of those who claim to know all the answers.

We confess that we have claimed to know the answers before, and we humbly repent.

Have mercy on us, for your son our Lord Jesus Christ's sake, and teach us to hold space in the wilderness for our fellow wanderers.

Give us the grace to create in this liminal space, to dance and make meaning and add color where there once was only darkness.

And all the while remind us that we have never been lost, that we are seen and known for every step of this long walk home, to the Honor and Glory of your Name, through Jesus Christ our Lord.

Amen.

Genesis

What's the point
of living in a garden
if in it flourishes fruit
I am forbidden to eat?

Indeed, the flesh is sweet.

False Gods

The old family story goes:
there was a beautiful dress,
treasured above all other adornments.
when it was dry-cleaned
it emerged from the machine
tragically torn to shreds.

The lesson I learned:
"don't love something too much
or God will take it from you."

If that's the case,
I'm terrified
of what God could do
for the way I have loved you.

Tough Love

Your love removes the tick behind my ear,
Blows out the match, and presses it
to the parasitic bulge.

You dig this needle into my skin,
but cross my heart and hope to die,
I won't let these tears fall.

Because maybe tough love is better
than no love at all.

Gloria in Excelsis

Glory to God in the highest,
whose mind we have not understood.

Lord God, gentle King, grant us that we may still know your presence as we wrestle.

We thank you that we do not have to choose between our questions and your love.

Lord Jesus Christ, God who suffers with us, Lord God, lamb to the slaughter:

Remind us that the ways of God are often unexpected,

And that the work of God is often slow;

Have mercy on us.

You are seated at the right hand of the Father, and you have heard our prayers in the night.

Be near to us in our humanity, and grant us hearts made more tender through pain.

For you alone are God-with-us, you alone are the Lord.

Jesus Christ, with the Holy Spirit, in the Glory of God the Father,

Remind us the darkness doesn't last forever.

Amen.

Church of the Water Falling

I have been un-churched,
de-churched, and re-churched,

but I have always belonged
to the church of the water falling,
ecumenical light cells dancing over smooth stones.

I have been baptized by a silent tide
like second skin rippling with slick moss.

And the water rushing, gushing, bleeding,
flinging itself from high towers,
perpetually giving itself away.

Beside the water falling
I have learned
again
to pray.

Sanctus

Holy Holy Holy, Lord God in which we have our Being,
Heaven and Earth are full of your glory.

Teach us to notice those sacred moments
Which might otherwise pass us by.

Train our senses to enjoy the world you have created for us
And teach our bodies to breathe deeply.

Remind us that we do not always have to be on guard
Because you hem us in behind and before.

Let your love be a soft landing for us,
A refuge from the cold and the rain.

And teach us to provide refuge to one another,
As if we each were host to angels.

Blessed is he who comes in the name of the Lord.

Hosanna in the Highest.

Amen.

Women's Work

Fallen onto straw, matted in blood
The Word was borne into the world
because there was a woman,
who broke herself to make room for more.

Perfume intermingled with
rusty nails was the
breeze from the body
because there was a woman
who washed his feet.

A tomb, discovered empty
spices scattered in haste
news for the brothers
because there was a woman
who rose early one morning.

His garb remains unblemished
By that holy wine, mixed with river life
every Sunday
because there is a woman
who washes the robes.

All the ways we
pretend not to see
that preaching the Gospel
has always been women's work.

No Christ But In Things

> *"And for the poet there are no ideas but in things."*
> — William Carlos Williams

No ideas but in things:
a chili recipe,
the lone garden zucchini,
and the way you patched up my jeans
with the holes in the knees.

No ideas but in leftovers
left in the fridge for me,
jumping my car
in the rain
on a Wednesday morning
when you had somewhere else to be.

No ideas but in birdfeeders,
front-row seating,
forehead kisses,
still not leaving.

And though you may not
have meant to be,
it's true, you have
been Christ to me.

Love, Again

For Jared Matthews

Tonight sounds like
leaves, rustling
lightbulbs, humming
sleeves, brushing

And the silent,
improbable feat of
lightning, striking
twice.

Be Fruitful and Multiply

The barren woman
raises laughter,
her daughter.

The unmothered
mothers sisters,
draws near and shares their breath.

The lonely
fathers steps towards water
for those who never thought
they could be made clean.

The mothered and the motherless
the fathered and the fatherless
are still breaking off bits of themselves.
Amazed, they find
there is more than enough
to go around.

Sabbath

It takes practice to
resurrect.

To sit so still you hear
your own breath return to
your body.

To notice beauty without
hating it isn't yours.

To drink the cup of knowledge
but stop when you've had your fill.

To acknowledge
that maybe these bones can break
but they can also heal.

www.ingramcontent.com/pod-product-compliance
Lightning Source LLC
Chambersburg PA
CBHW071802040426
42446CB00012B/2667